ALLEN COUNTY PUBLIC LIBRARY

3 1833 04286 3867

P9-AFY-542

ALLEN COUNTY PUBLIC LIBRARY

El Salvador
the people and culture

Greg Nickles

A Bobbie Kalman Book

The Lands, Peoples, and Cultures Series

 Crabtree Publishing Company

www.crabtreebooks.com

The Lands, Peoples, and Cultures Series

Created by Bobbie Kalman

Coordinating editor
Ellen Rodger

Assistant editor
P.A. Finlay

Production coordinator
Rosie Gowsell

Project development, photo research, and design
First Folio Resource Group, Inc.
  Erinn Banting
  Tom Dart
  Söğüt Y. Güleç
  Alana Lai
  Debbie Smith

Editing
Carolyn Black

Separations and film
Embassy Graphics

Printer
Worzalla Publishing Company

Consultants
Elisa de Carranza, Consulate General of El Salvador, Houston; Ana Cecilia Romero and Patricia Zepeda, Consulate of El Salvador, Toronto

Photographs
AP/Wide World Photo: p. 24 (left), p. 26, p. 27 (right); Piers Cavendish/Impact: p. 22 (left); Corbis/Magma Photo News Inc./Bettmann: p. 8, p. 9 (left), p. 13 (right); Corbis/Magma Photo News Inc./Joel W. Rogers: p. 9 (right); J.P. Courau/DDB Stock Photo: p. 12 (bottom), p. 24 (right), Lizzette Marenco de Dreyfus: p. 12 (top); Max Dreyfus: p. 16 (right); Carl Frank/Photo Researchers: p. 17 (bottom); Carlos Henriquez: p. 14 (left), p. 29; Mike Hutchison: p. 27 (left), p. 30 (top); Greg Johnston: cover, p. 10 (bottom), p. 20 (left); Alison M. Jones: p. 6 (left), p. 13 (left), p. 21 (bottom), p. 23 (both), p. 30 (bottom); Alyx Kellington/DDB Stock Photo: title page; North Wind Pictures: p. 6 (right), p. 7; Reuters/Luis Galdamez/Archive Photos: p. 15; Sean Sprague/Panos Pictures: p. 11 (both), p. 14 (right), p. 28 (left), p. 31; Tayacan/Panos Pictures: p. 22 (right); Anneke van Gijzen: p. 3, p. 19 (top), p. 28 (right); Eric Velado: p. 10 (top), p. 16 (left), p. 17 (top), p. 18, p. 19 (bottom), p. 20 (right), p. 21 (top), p. 25

Illustrations
Sylvie Bourbonnière, Anna Goodson Management: pp. 4–5
Dianne Eastman: icon
David Wysotski, Allure Illustrations: back cover

Cover: A boy holds up a bundle of lobsters and crabs from an outdoor fish market in La Libertad, in southern El Salvador.

Title page: A girl sits in a market stall where her family sells spices, noodles, and rice.

Icon: A *marimba*, which is a type of xylophone that has keys made from hollow gourds, appears at the head of each section.

Back cover: The *tigrillo*, or ocelot, is a small wildcat that lives in the mountainous regions of El Salvador.

Published by
Crabtree Publishing Company

PMB 16A,	612 Welland Avenue	73 Lime Walk
350 Fifth Avenue	St. Catharines	Headington
Suite 3308	Ontario, Canada	Oxford OX3 7AD
New York	L2M 5V6	United Kingdom
N.Y. 10118		

Copyright © 2002 CRABTREE PUBLISHING COMPANY. All rights reserved. No part of this publication may be reproduced, stored in a retrieval system or transmitted in any form or by any means, electronic, mechanical, photocopying, recording, or otherwise, without the prior written permission of Crabtree Publishing Company.

Cataloging in Publication Data

Nickles, Greg, 1969-
  El Salvador. The people and culture / Greg Nickles.
    p. cm. -- (The lands, peoples, and cultures series)
    Includes index.
    Summary: Introduces the religion, holidays and festivals, art, traditional and modern dance and music, language, and literature of El Salvador.
    ISBN 0-7787-9368-0 (RLB) -- ISBN 0-7787-9736-8 (pbk.)
    1. El Salvador--Social life and customs--21st century--Juvenile literature. 2. El Salvador--History--Juvenile literature. [1. El Salvador--Social life and customs.] I. Title. II. Series
    F1488.5 .N53 2002
    972.8405′2--dc21
                                        2001032530
                                        LC

Contents

A tale of the first human

Long ago, the ancient Mayan people lived in El Salvador. They told a story of a time when only plants and wild animals lived on the earth. The supreme being, Hunabku, and the other Mayan gods watched over these plants and animals. One day, the gods commanded the animals, "Call out our names and **worship** us, your creators and **ancestors**." The animals could only reply with noisy squawks, roars, growls, and honks.

"This is not good," Hunabku said to the other gods. "We must have creatures on this earth that can think and speak, so they can honor and serve us." All day and night, the gods debated how to make such creatures. Finally, the supreme Hunabku said, "Quickly, let us build our new creatures out of dirt before the magical hour of dawn arrives."

The gods finished making the dirt creatures at sunrise, and commanded, "Call out our names and worship us, your creators and ancestors." The dirt creatures spoke, but their words made no sense. Later, when it started to rain, the creatures turned into mud and were washed away.

"We must try our luck again," said mighty Hunabku. He asked the gods Ixpiyacoc and Ixmucané, the grandparents of **humanity**, for advice. They replied, "Why not make the creatures from wood?"

The gods worked all night. As the next day dawned, their skinny wooden creatures came to life. The gods grew excited watching them chatter and climb trees. "Call out our names and worship us," they commanded, but the creatures did not obey. Instead, they ran away to live with the other wild animals. Today, we call these creatures monkeys.

The gods were disappointed, but Hunabku encouraged them. "These creatures are much better than the ones we made from mud. With the knowledge we gained making them, we will finally build the creature we want."

Then, Hunabku said to Ah Mun, the god of corn, "Give me a tiny, golden kernel of corn." From the kernel, the gods very carefully molded another creation, which came to life at sunrise. This time, the creature moved, talked, and thought. When the gods commanded, it spoke their names and worshiped them. At last, Hunabku and the other gods were satisfied. Hunabku announced proudly, "We have created the first human on earth."

Conquest by Spain

The Spanish conquest began in El Salvador in 1524. Spanish soldiers, called *conquistadores*, arrived in sailing ships from Europe. They conquered the peoples they found and made them **subjects** and slaves of Spain. The Spaniards' ships, horses, steel armor, and weapons made them stronger warriors than El Salvador's Native peoples. By 1528, the leader of the *conquistadores* in El Salvador, Don Pedro de Alvarado, conquered the Pipíl.

In the name of the savior

After the conquest, El Salvador and other places in Central America became part of a Spanish province called Guatemala. Spanish settlers and merchants came to the province, bringing their culture and the Christian religion. Christians follow the teachings of Jesus Christ, whom they believe is the son of God and whom they call their **savior**. Spanish settlers used their word for savior, *salvador*, to name the region of El Salvador and its future **capital**, San Salvador.

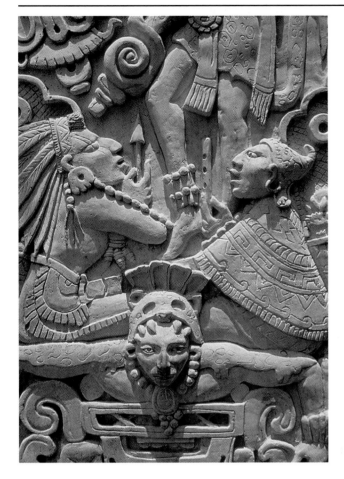

The Mayan ruins at San Andrés are decorated with intricate carvings that depict gods and goddesses, ancient leaders, and powerful warriors.

Many peoples have lived in El Salvador throughout the land's long history. The Olmec people built the first known civilization there 3,000 years ago. They created cities of stone that had large **step pyramids** and monumental sculptures. The Mayan people lived in El Salvador after the Olmecs. The Maya made important discoveries in writing, mathematics, and **astronomy**, and created very precise calendars. About 1,000 years ago, the Pipíl settled in El Salvador. They were skilled warriors who, like the Maya, knew a great deal about science and stone building.

During the 1500s, Don Pedro de Alvarado conquered Mexico and much of Central America, including present-day Guatemala, El Salvador, and Honduras.

Toward independence

Under Spanish rule, El Salvador's economy became based on agriculture. A few wealthy families who were originally from Spain established large farms, called **plantations**, where they grew sugar and **indigo**. These families also helped govern the province.

After nearly 300 years, the wealthy families wanted to rule Central America on their own, without Spain's help. Many workers and other local people also supported **independence** from Spain because they hoped it would improve their living conditions. Spain refused to grant their wish. In 1811, Salvadorans José Matías Delgado and his nephew Manuel José Arce began a **rebellion** against Spanish rule. The rebellion was soon crushed, but Delgado and Arce became heroes.

New countries

In 1821, the province of Guatemala broke away from Spain. Two years later, El Salvador, along with four other Central American countries, became part of the United Provinces of Central America. Political and religious differences soon divided the people of the United Provinces, and **civil war** erupted in 1827. The war ended in 1829, but the problems continued. The United Provinces broke apart in 1840, and El Salvador became its own country in 1841.

Native peoples fight back

Spanish rule greatly affected the Native peoples of El Salvador. Thousands died while fighting the Spanish during and after the conquest or while working as slaves on plantations. Others died of European diseases. The Spanish forced the remaining Native peoples to adopt the Spanish language and culture.

Salvadoran Anastasio Aquino led the Native peoples in a rebellion against the Spanish in 1833. Many non-Native people, tired of living in poverty, also fought in the rebellion. The rebels won the cities of Zacatecoluca and San Vicente, in the central part of the country, but government troops defeated them in the mountains. Aquino was put to death for treason, or crimes against his country. Today, many Salvadorans remember him as a great hero.

Struggle and civil war

Throughout the 1800s, wealthy Salvadoran families controlled El Salvador's government. By forcing small farmers out of business, they took over most of the country's farmland for their plantations. The *Catorce Familias*, or "Fourteen Families," became the most powerful people in the land. They made large fortunes growing and selling coffee beans and cotton.

Coming together

Increasingly, Salvadorans relied on the plantations for jobs. These jobs involved hard work, but the workers were not paid well. They began to blame the *Catorce Familias*. Some argued that **fertile** land should be taken away from the wealthy and given to the workers. Others took part in violent attacks to force the government to make changes.

In this photograph from 1931, people shop in a busy market in San Salvador.

Years of troubles

In 1929, a worldwide economic crisis, called the Great Depression, began. Thousands of Salvadorans lost their jobs because other countries stopped buying their crops. Led by **revolutionaries** such as Augustín Farabundo Martí, many Salvadorans rebelled against the government. The Salvadoran military took control of the country in 1931, partly to protect the *Catorce Familias*. The government ordered a massacre, later called *la matanza* or "the slaughter," to wipe out the rebels and their supporters. Up to 30,000 Salvadorans, mostly Native peoples, were murdered. Martí was executed, and surviving rebels went into hiding.

Military rule

Military leaders controlled El Salvador for most of the next 50 years. Although they encouraged new industries, many Salvadorans still suffered shortages of food, housing, and jobs.

The Soccer War

In 1969, El Salvador went to war with its neighbor Honduras. The conflict was called the Soccer War because it began right after the two countries played against each other in the World Cup soccer tournament. They fought the Soccer War over Salvadorans who had moved illegally into Honduras to find a better life. Honduras wanted El Salvador to take back the illegal **immigrants.** During the war's four days of heavy fighting, several thousand people were killed or injured.

The civil war

Since *la matanza*, rebels in El Salvador continued to plot against the government. In the 1970s, they formed a new army called the FMLN, or *Farabundo Martí Liberation National*. The FMLN pledged to take over the country, and end poverty and government corruption. They kidnapped members of the government and military, and held them for **ransom** to get money for their own army. They also killed hundreds of people who refused to support them. The government forces, in turn, killed many peasant supporters of the FMLN. In 1979, the conflict between the government and the FMLN erupted into civil war, during which tens of thousands of people were arrested, tortured, and killed.

A soldier fighting during the civil war carries his wounded friend to safer ground.

Americans protest against their government's military and financial support of the Salvadoran government's fight against FMLN rebels.

Peace at last

Slowly, the rebels' actions led to change. In 1983, El Salvador adopted a new constitution. One year later, elected politicians replaced military rulers. José Napoleón Duarte became president. In 1992, the government signed a peace agreement with the FMLN. The agreement promised that the poor would get land and FMLN members would help run the country. During the long war, over 75,000 people were killed and over one million fled to other countries for safety.

Building new lives

Today, millions of Salvadorans are grateful for the peace they have enjoyed since 1992. They are slowly rebuilding their country. Salvadorans hope that their leaders will keep the peace and make changes to improve their daily lives.

The Salvadorans

More than six million people live in El Salvador, although geographically it is the smallest country in Central America. It is one of the most densely populated countries in the world. Most Salvadorans crowd into cities and towns on the plains and highlands. Few people live in the mountainous countryside.

Both Spanish and Native

Many Spaniards who settled in El Salvador in the 1500s **intermarried** and had children with Native peoples. Today, more than 90 percent of El Salvador's population has mixed Spanish and Native ancestry. They speak Spanish and follow many Spanish traditions.

Dressed in a brightly colored headscarf and dress, a woman prepares to perform a traditional dance during a festival in Suchitoto, in central El Salvador.

Pineapples, coconuts, bananas, and other fresh fruit are for sale at this farmer's market in San Vicente, in central El Salvador.

A young boy plays on a dock near his family's boat in La Libertad, on the southern coast.

From Europe and the Middle East

A small number of Salvadorans have solely Spanish ancestry. These people usually belong to the country's wealthy families and make up two to five percent of the population. Another small number of Salvadorans are descendants of Palestinian, Jewish, and Lebanese immigrants who came to the country in the 1800s.

Native peoples

People estimate that around 60,000 Native people live in El Salvador, although no one is sure of the exact number. The reason for this uncertainty is that many Native peoples look similar to other Salvadorans. They have also adopted the Spanish language, styles of clothing, and customs, hoping to escape poor treatment and violence from other Salvadorans.

Pipíl survivors

Of the remaining groups of Native peoples in El Salvador, the Pipíl are the largest. The Pipíl live mainly in villages in the southwest part of the country, where they still preserve some of their culture. Some Pipíl continue to believe in their traditional gods of corn, rain, sun, wind, and earth. Others combine these beliefs with Christianity. They do traditional crafts such as weaving, pottery, and metalwork. Most Pipíl speak Spanish, but a few elders speak the Pipíl language, Nahuatl.

The Lenca people of eastern El Salvador are **descendants** of the ancient Maya. Little is known of the Lencas' traditions, which have nearly disappeared.

Salvadorans in other countries

Even though the civil war ended in 1992, many Salvadorans who fled the fighting remain in other countries. There, they have found jobs and homes. Many send money to their relatives in El Salvador to help them pay for food, clothes, and shelter.

A sister and brother visit their grandfather on his farm near San Salvador. About 30 percent of Salvadorans are farmers.

Religion and worship

Religion has always been an important part of community life in El Salvador. Prayer comforts worshipers, especially during the country's hard times. Sometimes, churches offer basic medical care, food, and clothing to people who do not have much money. They also help set up housing developments and craft shops where many Salvadorans live and work.

The Christian religion

Almost all Salvadorans are Christians. Their religion is based on the teachings of Jesus Christ and on the holy book called the Bible. Christians believe that Christ performed miracles such as healing the sick and returning to life after he was crucified, or put to death on a cross.

(left) Small ceramic statues and paintings depicting saints are sold outside a church in Sonsonate, in western El Salvador.

(below) The cathedral in Santa Ana, in western El Salvador, was built in 1905. It is one of the oldest Roman Catholic churches in the country.

Many of El Salvador's towns and villages have small stone churches where people gather and pray.

Catholics and Protestants

Most Salvadorans are Roman Catholics. Roman Catholicism is a **denomination** of Christianity that is about 2,000 years old. The Spanish introduced Roman Catholicism to El Salvador in the 1500s. In each town and city, they built churches and **shrines** devoted to saints, or holy people.

After the 1980s, another denomination of Christianity called Protestantism became popular. Most Salvadoran Protestants are former Roman Catholics.

Politics and poverty

Many Salvadoran religious leaders have been active in politics. Some have led people to organize themselves in their fight against poverty. This teaching began in the late 1960s and is called "liberation theology." Rather than watch silently as innocent Salvadorans were arrested and killed by the military during the civil war, Roman Catholic priests and nuns spoke out against the government. In response, the military killed many of them.

Archbishop Romero

In 1977, Oscar Anulfo Romero (1917–1980) became San Salvador's **archbishop**. Romero knew the military government committed crimes against innocent Salvadorans. He decided to take a stand after the government killed his friend, the priest Retulio Grande. Romero began publishing the names of people who had "disappeared," or were secretly arrested by the police. He also preached against violence to his followers each Sunday, urging government soldiers not to kill. As people around the world heard of the suffering in El Salvador, Romero became known as "the voice of the voiceless."

Romero's actions earned him powerful enemies. In 1980, he was murdered while leading a Sunday church service. At his funeral, many of his followers were shot and killed. Most people believe that the military sent the murderers, who were never caught. Today, Archbishop Romero is the country's most beloved hero. The Catholic Church is in the process of canonizing him, or making him a saint.

13

Holidays and festivals

On May 6, people in the town of Panchimalco, in central El Salvador, celebrate **Las Palmas. Las Palmas** *is a festival that honors the Virgen de Fatima, a saint who is believed to have performed many miracles.*

Salvadorans have many holidays and festivals. Most are religious events. Others celebrate the harvest, the anniversary of an important day in history, or the arts. Costumes, parades, sports, concerts, and dancing are all part of the festivities.

La Navidad

Christians in El Salvador celebrate the birth of Jesus Christ with *La Navidad*, or Christmas, on December 25. In the days leading up to *La Navidad*, they set up *nacimientos*, or Nativity scenes, in churches and homes. *Nacimientos* show the baby Jesus and his parents, Mary and Joseph, in the stable where Jesus was born.

La Noche Buena

On *La Noche Buena*, "The Good Night" before *La Navidad*, families go to church. There, they sing carols and watch the children's Christmas **pageant**. Then, everyone returns home for a party. Children enjoy the feasting, music, and dancing, but are anxious to go to bed so *El Niño Dios*, the baby Jesus, can bring them a present. They awake later that night or early in the morning to find a small gift under their pillow. *La Navidad* is a quiet day for families to relax and, often, to go to the beach. Children receive gifts again on January 6, the Epiphany. This holiday marks the visit of three kings who brought gifts for the baby Jesus.

Beginning December 15, special parades called **posadas** *re-enact the journey to the stable where Jesus was born. Children walk through their town or neighborhood carrying images of Mary and Joseph, stopping at each house to sing carols to the* **nacimientos.** *The* **posada** *grows larger until it reaches the last house, where everyone stays for a party.*

Honoring Christ's death

The Christian holiday of *Pascua*, or Easter, falls in March or April. *Pascua* marks the death and **resurrection** of Christ. On Good Friday, the day that Christ died, Salvadorans join in a solemn procession to church, carrying a painting or statue of Christ. At church, the priest leads songs and prayers. Then, worshipers light candles and guard a statue of Christ until nightfall.

Returning to life

On Easter Sunday, the day when Christ rose from the dead, a joyful procession carries an image of the risen Christ through the streets. The priest leads a special service, blessing Christ's followers and sometimes their animals. At home, children hunt for eggs and treats. A favorite trick is to cut the top off a raw egg, pour out the yolk, fill the egg with confetti, and then crack it over someone's head as a surprise. *Pascua* ends with feasting and parties.

Palm Sunday falls one week before Easter Sunday. Worshipers carrying palm branches blessed by the priest march in a procession with a statue of Christ.

San Miguel's *fiesta*

Every city, town, and village in El Salvador holds its own annual *fiesta*, or festival, to honor its patron saint. Roman Catholics believe that their patron saint protects them. A major focus of the *fiesta* in San Miguel, in eastern El Salvador, is a statue of its patron saint, Nuestra Señora de la Paz. The people of San Miguel believe this statue saved the city from an eruption of the nearby Chaparrastique volcano in 1787. The residents placed the statue at the door of their **cathedral** during the eruption and prayed for protection. The city was not destroyed, and residents have celebrated their *fiesta* ever since.

El Quince de Septiembre

Each year, Salvadorans and other Central Americans celebrate their independence from Spain on *El Quince de Septiembre*, or "The Fifteenth of September." In the week before this holiday, school children paint portraits and sing songs about the revolution against Spain. Then, on September 15, they parade through the streets with school marching bands. Soldiers march beside tanks; planes and helicopters fly overhead; and politicians give patriotic speeches.

Day of the Dead

In San Salvador, children celebrate Halloween on October 31 by going from door to door saying, "*Queremos dulces,*" or "We want candy," and by throwing eggs. The next day, they must clean up the mess they made! November 1 marks *El Día de los Muertos*, or "The Day of the Dead." People say that the spirits of dead loved ones return to earth on that day, so it is important for families to tidy their loved ones' graves. People leave gifts of flowers on the graves and eat special honey and corn flour cakes called *hoguelas de maiz* while visiting the cemetery.

Family traditions

Cousins wait for one of the many rides at a carnival in San Salvador to begin.

The bonds between Salvadoran children, parents, grandparents, aunts, uncles, and cousins are very strong. Many relatives live together, all doing chores and taking care of one another. Families also celebrate special occasions, such as births and birthdays, with one another, enjoying large meals, music, and dancing.

A new baby

Christian families welcome a new baby into their religion with a baptism. In a baptism ceremony, holy water is sprinkled on a baby's head. While some baptisms occur at church, many others take place at home, where the family holds a large party afterward. The parents choose *padrinos*, or godparents, for their child. The *padrinos* are usually family friends who promise to help take care of the child and his or her religious education.

Folk beliefs

Salvadorans have many folk beliefs surrounding the care of both a new baby and his or her mother. For example, neither the baby nor the mother is supposed to leave home for 40 days after the birth, for fear that they will become ill.

Some people believe that a father should hold his baby when he comes home from work. If he forgets, the baby may develop a nasty case of *pujos*, or hiccups! To prevent this, the father runs outside to work up a sweat. When he comes home, he holds the baby so it feels his sweat. People believe that the sweat keeps the baby from becoming ill.

The *curandera*

In the countryside and occasionally in cities, people sometimes take sick children to a *curandera*, a woman who practices a kind of folk medicine called *brujería*. The *curandera*'s cure may involve holding the child upside down by his or her feet, or rubbing a paste of garlic on the child's body.

During Roman Catholic services, people take communion. Children make their First Communion when they are seven or eight years old.

Happy birthday!

Salvadorans make sure that birthdays start off on a happy note. Family members often rise early in the morning, so they can wake the birthday person with a loud chorus of "Happy Birthday." A band is sometimes hired to play along. Later that day, family and friends throw a party with sandwiches, cake, and dancing. At a child's party, children put on a blindfold and take turns trying to burst a *piñata* with a stick. A *piñata* is a **papier-mâché** animal that is hung in the air. Once the *piñata* bursts open, candies stored inside fall to the ground. Everyone scrambles to pick them up.

Reaching fifteen

When a Salvadoran girl turns fifteen years old, she celebrates her *quinceañera*. This party marks her passage into adulthood. She wears a special dress for the occasion. Accompanied by fourteen girlfriends, she goes to church for a ceremony in which she offers thanks for reaching adulthood. Afterward, her family holds a party and a dance.

Family and friends at a birthday party gather around a house that the children made as a gift.

Elisa's arms are getting tired from carrying these watermelons home from the market. Watermelons are a favorite treat at birthday parties.

Music and dance

Across El Salvador, dance and music are important at home, at church, and during celebrations. Many people, especially in the countryside, enjoy traditional styles of dance and music. In towns and cities, rock and salsa music are popular. The country's symphony orchestra, *La Orquesta Simfónica de El Salvador*, performs classical music.

Very old instruments

Archaeologists, digging in the ruins of ancient Salvadoran settlements, uncovered many types of instruments that folk musicians still play today. These include *pitos*, which are high-pitched whistles, *chirimías* pipes, and drums such as the large, booming *tambor* and the smaller, tapping *tun*.

Strings and percussion

People from other countries introduced many instruments that Salvadoran musicians now play. Spanish settlers introduced the guitar, which became one of the most important instruments in Salvadoran folk music.

Another common folk instrument, the *marimba*, is like a wooden xylophone. The keys of a *marimba* are made from hollow **gourds**. A musician strikes the gourds using a padded stick to make a chiming sound. Usually, only one person plays a *marimba*, but some *marimbas* are so large that nine musicians can play them at once!

A *marimba* festival

Each year, San Miguel holds a festival to celebrate *marimba* music. The festival lasts several days. Bands with *marimbas* and other instruments perform on the city's main streets. Crowds of people gather around to listen and dance.

*Children play different traditional instruments, such as **castanets**, which are clapped together with the thumb and fingers; **maracas**, which are shaken; **marimbas**; and a **tambor**.*

Two girls, dressed in fancy costumes, perform a traditional dance for their classmates at a school assembly.

Singing *canciónes*

Canción is Spanish for "song." *Canciónes* are one of the most common types of folk music performed in El Salvador. Traditional *canciónes* describe Salvadorans' daily lives or tell about important events that took place in the country. Many *canciónes* are funny songs or songs of love. Singers perform *canciónes* at home with family and friends, or at public events, where everyone is invited to sing along.

Traditional dances

Salvadorans perform traditional dances at festivals or parties. The traditional *cúmbia* has short, sliding steps that are danced to the fast rhythm of *cúmbia* music. Other traditional dances come from the rain dances of the ancient Mayan people.

"El Carbonero," or "the charcoal man," is a popular traditional dance in El Salvador. People dance around a knife, called la cuma, that workers use to cut charcoal into pieces and a sack that people use to carry charcoal to the market.

Arts and crafts

Salvadorans create a wide range of handicrafts and folk art, from everyday tools and furniture to clothing, blankets, and toys. They decorate this art in both Native and Spanish styles, with bright colors and patterns.

Making handicrafts

It is not unusual for all the **artisans** of one village to make the same kind of handicraft. The village of Concepción Quezaltepeque, in the north, is a hammock-making center. Artisans in Sesuntepeque, in the central part of the country, specialize in weaving palm-leaf hats. **Wicker** workshops line the main street of Nahuizalco, in the west. Rope, pottery, fabrics, jewelry, and hand-painted crosses and cards are other products that an artisan may make. Artisans take their products to the market in the nearest town or city to sell or trade them for other goods.

A woman carefully paints a Mayan symbol on a ceramic mug. The Maya used combinations of symbols depicting animals and people to represent different words.

A woman holds up a brightly colored woven blanket that was made in Panchimalco.

Sorpresas

Salvadorans enjoy making small *sorpresas*, or "surprises." These beautiful handicrafts are a specialty of the town of Ilobasco, in the country's east. *Sorpresas* are shaped like eggs or walnuts. They open to reveal a surprise called a *típica*. The *típica* is a little scene of daily village life, made of tiny clay figures. Many girls over the age of twelve go to classes to learn how to paint *sorpresas*.

Working together

In many places, artisans' workshops are cooperatives. Cooperatives are businesses owned by all the workers. The workers share equally in any decisions and profits that are made. Cooperatives have improved the lives of many Salvadorans. Workers earn money while learning new skills.

Painting and drawing

El Salvador's artists often use traditional colors, patterns, and ideas in their work. The art of Fernando Llort (1949–) is famous around the world. Born in San Salvador, Llort moved to the northern village of La Palma in 1972. There, he began painting childlike, colorful scenes of villages, people, animals, and *campesinos*, or images of Christ. He set up a cooperative workshop, where he taught local people to paint in his style. The artwork of Llort's cooperative grew so popular that, today, most of La Palma's residents make their living from it. They closely follow Llort's style, painting images on everything from crosses to key rings.

Art and politics

Before and during the civil war, some Salvadoran artists created pieces of art that criticized the government and its military rulers. Revolutionary posters, banners, and graffiti became a common sight on the streets of Salvadoran cities. After the war, new posters gradually covered the wartime art. Politics is still an important subject of Salvadoran art.

Fernando Llort works on one of his paintings at his studio in La Palma. Today, more than 3,000 artisans in La Palma paint in Llort's style.

A brightly colored mural showing a scene from the countryside decorates the side of this home.

21

Life in the countryside

Carts pulled by bulls are used to transport water from a well to a village near San Miguel.

In many ways, life in El Salvador's countryside is the same as it has been for a hundred years. Large families often live together in small homes. Most families in the countryside do not have vehicles, indoor plumbing, or electricity. More Salvadorans live in the countryside than in the city.

Under the volcano

Some families live on farms and in small communities on the slopes of El Salvador's mountains and volcanoes. Unpaved roads connect these farms and villages to surrounding towns and cities. People travel on foot, by bicycle or mule, or in a cart drawn by horses, oxen, or other farm animals. If they are traveling long distances, people usually take a bus.

In a village

A *plaza* is often at the center of a village. A *plaza* is an open square lined with trees and benches. People meet there to relax with family and friends, or to take part in community events. A church usually stands beside the *plaza*, with a school nearby. Houses cluster around the center of the village.

The smallest villages have just a few houses and no churches or schools. A traveling priest goes from village to village, performing religious ceremonies for the people who live there. For special events, such as baptisms and weddings, the priest may perform services for many families at the same time. If there is no school in a village, children may walk far distances to attend classes in a neighboring village. Some children stay home to work.

Working in the fields

Many people from the countryside work on plantations. They spend long hours growing and harvesting the landowners' crops, especially coffee, for little pay. At harvest time, everyone, from children to grandparents, works in the fields. Other farmers, called subsistence farmers, tend their own land, barely growing enough to feed themselves and their families.

Children practice their spelling at a school in Suchitoto. In the countryside, many children have their classes outside.

The roof of this couple's home, in La Libertad, is made from red tiles.

Country homes

Farmers and other workers in the countryside often live in small houses built from wood or from sun-dried bricks made of clay and straw. Roofs are made of **thatch** or red tiles. A *choza* or *rancho*, made of branches woven together, is another common type of home. A protective layer of dried mud covers its walls. Inside the home are a few pieces of furniture. Hanging blankets, instead of walls, often divide one or two rooms. Light comes from oil lamps or candles. Outside, people cook in wood-burning ovens. They get water from a nearby well or stream, where they also bathe and wash clothes. They love listening to the radio and watching television, which they power with car batteries.

The few wealthy landowners in El Salvador live in *villas*, or estates filled with every convenience and luxury. Some of these houses are very old. Others are similar to new mansions in North America.

Many families in small villages wash their clothes in nearby rivers and streams.

Life in the cities

El Salvador's cities are busy with people, special events, businesses, and interesting things to see. The cities are very crowded, especially San Salvador, and there are not enough homes for everyone. Despite this housing shortage, people continue to move to cities from the countryside. They are searching for better schools, hospitals, and jobs.

City homes

Families in the city have fewer children than those in the countryside. Most people live in apartment buildings or small, simple houses with basic appliances and a few pieces of furniture. The wealthiest families live in expensive neighborhoods, in luxurious homes with pools and gardens.

Traffic is backed up along a street in San Salvador, El Salvador's busy capital.

Santa Ana's city hall, like most of the city's important buildings, stands in the central plaza.

On the outskirts

Hundreds of thousands of people live on the outskirts of cities. They make their homes in older buildings or single-room houses built from cement blocks and scraps of lumber, plastic, or cardboard. Most do not have electricity, but some people hook wires into nearby city power lines. They get water from a faucet in the street, which the neighbors share.

Work and play

People in cities have many different jobs. Some work in factories or on construction sites. Others work in government offices, stores, restaurants, or hotels. After a long day, they are ready to relax and have fun. They get together with family and friends to eat, talk, listen to the radio, and play music. They also hang out at the *plaza*; go to *comedores*, or cafés; watch movies; or relax at nightclubs with live music and dancing.

Going to school

The school year lasts from late January to October. Children begin each day standing in *formación*, or "formation," as their teacher makes sure they are neatly dressed. Children study subjects such as language, math, geography, and science. Beginning in grade seven, they also learn English. After school, students work, play with friends, or do their homework.

There are more than 200 stores in this shopping mall in Santa Tecla, a suburb of San Salvador.

Busy markets

Most Salvadorans shop for produce or meat daily in *mercados*, or outdoor markets. Every few days, they stock up on basic foods such as corn, beans, and rice. The largest market sits in the center of town and sprawls across several streets. There, vendors set up stalls filled with all sorts of colorful goods, including fresh food, flowers, clothes, toys, books, and electronics. Women are often in charge of shopping for their family. To get through the market crowds, they sometimes carry their purchases on their heads in *canastos*, or wicker baskets.

Indoor shopping

Some Salvadorans shop for food and other necessities at their city's department stores, supermarkets, and malls, which are similar to those found in the United States and Canada. Prices are much higher than at the street markets, but there are many popular products, especially American clothing, that are hard to find elsewhere.

Sports and pastimes

After a hard day's work, Salvadorans like to have fun! They enjoy sports, games, music, dancing, and good food.

At the *plaza*

El Salvador's climate is warm, so people spend time outdoors throughout the year. The *plaza* is one of their favorite places to visit. Beautiful trees, flowers, statues, and fountains decorate the *plaza*. Some Salvadorans spend hours there, reading, taking a nap, playing sports, talking to friends, or people-watching.

On the beach

The beach is another popular place to relax, play, or have a picnic. People from all over the country pack El Salvador's lakeside and seaside beaches. Sunday afternoons, as well as holidays such as Christmas and Easter, are favorite times to go to the beach or to swim in one of the hundreds of rivers that flow through the countryside.

(top) People swim and enjoy the warm weather during their Easter vacation at Majahual Beach, on the Pacific coast.

*In the game **paolo encebado**, or "greasy wood," children try to get to the top of a slippery pole by standing on each other's shoulders. The first child to reach the top wins a small sack full of money.*

Fútbol

Fútbol, or soccer, is the most popular sport in El Salvador. Both children and adults love to play *fútbol* in parks, *plazas*, or on streets where there is little traffic. If players cannot afford a soccer ball, they sometimes make one out of a nylon stocking stuffed with rags.

Children's games

Salvadoran children love playing *mica* and *escondelero*. *Mica* is a game of tag. *Escondelero* is a combination of tag and hide-and-seek, played with a ball. To play *escondelero*, place a ball on the ground and choose one person to guard it. All the other players hide. While the guard searches for the hidden players, they try to sneak up and kick the ball. If the guard tags the other players, they are captured. If someone kicks the ball, the players are freed. The game ends when everyone is captured.

Basketball is a popular Salvadoran sport, especially in schools. Crowds of spectators often sing or play instruments to cheer on their team.

Repeat after me....

Like many other people in the world, Salvadorans speak Spanish. If you were in the *plaza* of a Salvadoran city, you might hear some of the words below:

English	Spanish
Good day, good morning	*Buenas dias*
Hello	*Hola*
Thank you	*Gracias*
You're welcome or "it was nothing"	*De nada*
Yes	*Si*
No	*No*
Kid or young boy (from the word for bug)	*Bicho*
Hey! or No way!	*Noombre!*
Holy cow!	*Puchica!*

The flavors of El Salvador

Salvadorans usually eat traditional foods made from eggs, cheese, corn, beans, squash, and rice. They also eat a lot of fruit. Meat and seafood are more expensive, so Salvadorans eat them less often. People in cities enjoy fast foods, such as hamburgers and pizzas, as well as a Salvadoran snack called a *pupusa*.

Tortillas everywhere!

Tortillas are as common in El Salvador as bread and potatoes are in North America. These round, flat cakes are made from corn. Some families take their corn to a nearby *molino*, or grinder, who crushes it into a fine flour. The family uses this flour to make *tortilla* dough. Other families make *masa*, or corn dough, by softening the kernels in water and then pounding them into a sticky mash with a grinding stone. They shape the dough into *tortillas* and cook them on a hot clay grill. When brown flecks cover the *tortillas*, they are ready to be served.

Mealtime

Salvadorans eat three main meals a day. *Desayuno*, or breakfast, is between 6:00 and 7:30 in the morning. Most people eat a *tortilla* soaked in warm milk with a cup of coffee and some fruit. *Almuerzo*, the midday meal, is often large. After a bowl of soup, people eat *tortillas* with rice, beans, corn, meat, or fish. People in the countryside might take a break, or *siesta*, after eating such a large meal. For *la cena*, or supper, people usually eat *tortillas* and vegetables. *La cena* is often late in the evening. People also eat many tropical fruits from El Salvador's Pacific shore. These include mangoes, avocados, and coconuts, as well as the sweet *nance*, a kind of red or yellow berry, and the juicy *jocote*, a fruit similar to a plum.

Pupusas

Pupusas are a Salvadoran specialty. They can be a snack or part of a larger meal. *Pupusas* are like fat *tortillas*, made of *masa* stuffed with cheese, pork, or beans. *Pupusas* are topped with *curtido*, a colorful mixture of pickled cabbage, carrots, and onions. People buy *pupusas* from streetside stands and shops called *pupuserías*. The snacks are so popular that 4:00 in the afternoon, the time that most *pupuserías* open, is known as "*pupusa* time."

*(above) A girl makes **tortillas** over a fire in her home on Monte Cristo, an island off the southern coast of El Salvador.*

*(right) A family sits down together to enjoy a meal of **tortillas**, corn, meat, and a refreshing glass of lemonade.*

Dried beans, spices, and corn are used in many Salvadoran dishes.

Fry, fry again

Salvadorans eat a lot of beans, including black beans and a red bean that is similar to a kidney bean, but smaller. They boil the dry beans until they are soft, mash them into a paste, and fry them. After a meal, they store the leftover bean paste in a clay pot. The longer it stays in the pot, the more flavorful it becomes. For the next meal, they fry the bean paste again. *Frijoles refritos*, or refried beans, mixed with vegetables, corn, and rice make a tasty meal.

Drinking beans and coconuts

The drink that El Salvador is best known for is coffee. For over a hundred years, the country has been one of the leading producers of coffee beans in the world. Hot chocolate, invented by the ancient Mayan people, is another favorite hot drink. *Horchata* is also popular. It is a sweet drink that is sometimes made of ground squash seeds, corn, and water, and sometimes made of sugar, cinnamon, and starchy water in which rice has soaked. Salvadorans also enjoy fresh fruit drinks. *Licuados* are made from fruit and milk, while *refrescos* are made from coconut and tropical fruit juices.

Bananos en gloria

Bananas are a favorite fruit in El Salvador. They are the main ingredient in this dish, called *bananos en gloria* or "glory bananas." You can serve *bananos en gloria* with refried red beans and sour cream, or eat them on their own for dessert.

It is easy to prepare *bananos en gloria* with an adult's help. You need:
a skillet
a knife
1 tablespoon (15 ml) butter or margarine
10 ripe bananas
1 tablespoon (15 ml) sugar
1 teaspoon (5 ml) cinnamon

1. Melt the butter or margarine in a hot skillet.

2. Peel and slice the bananas. Place them in the skillet.

3. Add the sugar and cinnamon.

4. Cover the skillet and lower the heat.

5. Cook for 10 to 12 minutes, until the bananas are golden brown and have a honey-like texture. This recipe serves five to ten people.

A special visit

Julia was excited. Her cousins, aunt, and uncle would be at her apartment any minute. Her father, who was tuning his guitar, spotted her waiting by the door … again. "Julia," he said, "I told you to do your geography homework until they arrive."

(top) Julia can hardly wait to get home from school to see her aunt, uncle, and cousins.

(below) Julia's uncle owns a cattle farm. Her cousins help him with the daily chores after school.

"But, Tata, I already spent the afternoon with my study group. It's the eve of Independence!" Tata turned to Mamá, who was setting the table with delicious food for their guests. Mamá said, "Oh, let her skip the books, just this once." Julia smiled at her mother, who winked back. "All right," Tata said finally, "but only if I get to eat your delicious *tortillas*."

Julia laughed as she took the grinding stones and mashed the kernels of corn. Her piping hot *tortillas* would be the finishing touch to Mamá's feast. As Julia worked over the hot griddle, she thought about their guests. "Mamá," she asked, "why did Tía Alicia and Tío José stay in the village while we moved to the city?"

"Our families have been farmers for many generations, so it's hard for José, or anybody, to leave," Mamá answered as she chopped tomatoes. "But your Tata and I heard about factory jobs in the city. We thought that coming here would mean a better life."

While shopping at the market for ingredients for dinner, Julia's mother spots fresh avocados.

Just then, Julia heard loud voices in the hall, and the door burst open. Julia's two younger brothers ran in, leading her aunt and uncle, and their four children. What a commotion! The tiny apartment was instantly packed with people. Alicia and José rushed to hug and kiss Julia, Mamá, and Tata. "Happy *Quince de Septiembre!*" each of them exclaimed.

After their greetings, José tried to find a spot for his *tambor* that was safe from all the children running around, laughing and playing. "I think my drum will be fine right here, close to these delicious-smelling *pupusas!*" he said, sitting down right in front of them.

"We had better start the meal before my brother eats all the appetizers!" Mamá joked. There was not enough room at the table for everyone to eat at the same time, so Julia's family ate in shifts. The wonderful meal included rice, squash, beans, chicken, all the *pupusas* they could eat, and for dessert, fresh fruit.

After dinner, Julia's brothers and cousins ran into the hallway for a noisy game of *mica*. Julia stayed behind to listen to the adults' conversation. "We don't have much here, but it's better than before," Tata was saying. "If you like, José, I can put in a good word for you at the factory. My godfather is a foreman there. He'll find you a job if you want one."

"We love living in the countryside," José replied, "but even though more land is being given to regular farmers like us, it's hard to make ends meet."

"If there is work and a place to live, we'll move to the city," Tía Alicia said.

"Then it's settled," Mamá said, smiling at her brother. "I can't wait to have you here to stay."

"What's all this talk about work on the eve of our holiday?" Tata cried, taking out his guitar. "Tonight we dance! And tomorrow, parades, speeches, and fireworks!" José grabbed his *tambor.* Julia smiled, happy to hear the two men play together again. As Julia's brothers and cousins came in from the hall, they joined in the singing, dancing, and laughing, until they all fell asleep, one by one.

Glossary

ancestor A person from whom one is descended

archaeologist A person who studies the past by looking at buildings and artifacts

archbishop The leader of a group of churches in a certain region

artisan A skilled craftsperson

astronomy The study of the stars and planets

capital A city where the government of a state or country is located

cathedral A large church

civil war A war between different groups of people or areas within a country

denomination A religious group within a faith

descendant A person who can trace his or her family roots to a certain family or group

fertile Able to produce abundant crops or vegetation

gourd The hard-shelled fruit of certain vines, which is dried to make musical instruments

harass To irritate or torment

humanity The human race

immigrant A person who settles in another country

independence The state of not being governed by a foreign power

indigo A plant that is used to make a blue dye

intermarry To marry someone from another culture or background

pageant A play that shows a historical event

papier-mâché Shreds of paper mixed with glue that are molded into shapes, dried, and painted

plantation A large farm on which crops, such as cotton, coffee, and sugar, are grown

ransom Payment for the release of a person

rebellion An uprising against a government

resurrection Rising from the dead or coming back to life

revolutionary A person who brings about or supports the overthrow or replacement of a government

savior A person who rescues another from harm or danger

shrine A small area or structure dedicated to a god or saint

step pyramid A four-sided structure with a rectangular base that ancient peoples used as a burial place

subject A person under the power of a leader or nation

thatch Plants, such as reeds or hay, woven together to make a roof

wicker A flexible plant branch that is woven into baskets or furniture

worship To honor or respect a god

Index